BE STILL AND BE BOLD

BE STILL AND BE BOLD

31 Meditations for Trauma Survivors

LORI A. PETERS

Lori A. Peters, MS LPC NCC CCTP-II

Credits.
Cover Art: iStock
Editing: Aden Nichols
Interior and Cover Layout Pickawoowoo Publishing Group

ISBN 978-1-7378851-0-8 (PAPERBACK)
ISBN 978-1-737-8851-1-5 (EBOOK)

Contents

31 Days of Going Inward to Grow Outward

INTRODUCTION

When you're a trauma survivor, getting through the day is a victory. Imagining getting through a month can be daunting. Each day can bring its own set of fears and triggers, even for those who are well into their recovery. Having an arsenal of coping tools goes a long way to strengthen the boundary between resilience and victimhood. Not dissimilar to someone recovering from substance abuse, a trauma survivor can wake up every day with a desire to retreat and return to what's been comfortable and safe. It's understandable considering all that has happened to them. Though it may be tempting to stay with what makes us feel comfortable, in the long run we can wind up doing more damage to ourselves. Staying comfortable prevents growth, and ultimately, healing. Healing involves taking risks because we will have to eventually confront what hurts us along with all the associated feelings and thoughts. It is possible to look into the mirror and say, "Yup, shit happened to me, but I survived and I'm safe now. Here's how I'm going to get through the day." I am living proof of that.

That is where this book comes in. My hope is this book will be an extra tool in your toolkit to keep you grounded, feeling safe and acting in a functional way. It's been said that it takes 21 days for something to become a habit. Let's extend that to 30 and see what can happen in a month while reading this book. It is filled with thoughtful and positive meditations that will encourage and uplift you. It may also get you thinking in a new way which keeps the brain sharp and helps you grow.

There is no particular order to this book, so start wherever you'd like. I purposely made it that way because healing is not linear. On some days, you may feel like you're making progress. On others, you may feel like you're at Day One. Also, if you don't feel like reading a passage on any given day, that's OK too. It is important that trauma survivors have choice, which is something we did not have during our traumatic experiences. Please read this whenever and however it suits you.

Also, because there is no particular order to this book, you will find sections that may repeat themselves to accommodate the reader's reading preferences, such as choosing to start in the middle or end of the book as opposed to the beginning. Repetition also aids in mastery of concepts. Research shows it can take anywhere between 6 and 20 times of repeating something before it sticks.

At the end of each meditation will be a section entitled *An Invitation to Act* in which you will be invited to take some concrete steps to further your recovery. I specifically chose the word 'invitation' to give you, the reader, the space to decide if you're ready to act. You may not be ready, and that's OK. Or, maybe the steps I'm suggesting are not right for you for one reason or another. And that's OK too. Each section is an encouragement.

This book is not a cure-all but a portal to another chapter of your recovery story. I understand readers from all points of the trauma recovery spectrum may be reading this. Your traumatic incident may have happened very recently, or it may have happened years or decades ago. Regardless of when the event happened, you are cautioned that some of the meditations may trigger you. Because of that distinct possibility, I strongly encourage you to seek out a competent and trauma-focused mental health professional to help you navigate whatever you may experience. Such a professional will help you develop strategies so you can cope with whatever thoughts and feelings that may arise, whether it's from reading this book or living your life every day.

So, you may be wondering who I am and why I've written this book. To put it simply, I am just like you. I am a survivor, now thriver. I have survived childhood, relational, medical, racial and spiritual trauma. I continue to struggle with cComplex PTSD, anxiety and depression. My ongoing process of healing has given me the unique opportunity to become a therapist and more recently, an intuition and resilience coach. I have benefitted from several items in my coping toolkit – therapy, writing, meditation and exercise to name a few. Now, I want to share some of what's been helpful to me with whoever is receptive to the information.

I hope you will take your time while reading this book, process whatever comes up for you and reread it again if you find something meaningful. Take each day one moment at a time. Sometimes, in that moment, if all you can do is breathe, then so be it. You'll get through. You've made it this far, so keep going.

I

RESILIENCE

We have the opportunity to grow stronger whenever change occurs, regardless of whether it's a good or bad change. We have the chance to display resilience by bouncing back after every negative circumstance. Resilience is rooted in the hope things will be better.

You have already displayed resilience – you are here, wherever here is, and you're reading this book that will assist you on your journey to a changed you, someone who can survive and thrive. You have weathered situations no one else has. ***You have survived.***

If you're coming off a battle for your life, you probably don't feel strong. The fight may have been beaten out of you, literally. You may wonder if you have what it takes to bounce back. These are all areas you'll have to explore.

LET'S TAKE THAT FIRST STEP TOGETHER.

An Invitation to Act

1. *Think about what resilience means for you. If you have a journal, you may want to write a few things down or list a few bullet points.*
2. *Ask yourself if you feel resilient. If the answer is yes, list what makes you feel that way. If the answer is no, ask yourself what you think you need in order to feel resilient. Be honest with yourself.*

2

MENTAL

To examine how far we've come, we need to gauge our mental, physical, emotional and spiritual growth. I'll be asking you to dig deep and be honest with yourself as you do that over the next few meditations and beyond. Honesty is the first step in self-awareness.

How are you doing mentally? What sort of thoughts are you having? Are they pushing you into a more positive direction or keeping you stagnant? The stories we tell ourselves – our thoughts – have a strong impact on how we view ourselves and others. What we think affects how we feel and behave. Mind, body and spirit are connected. If you've been thinking you can't make it because you're worthless, stupid and lazy, well, guess what? Odds are those thoughts will become a self-fulfilling prophecy. It took me years to drown out my dad's verbal abuse. He'd often call me stupid, claiming I'd never amount to anything. The seed of doubt he planted prevented me from pushing myself into areas that would've benefitted me. A small example is when I passed up the opportunity to enter a writing contest in high school. I decided from the very beginning that I'd never write anything worth anyone's time to read, so I never entered the contest, though I was encouraged to do so by my English teacher. I still regret that today. Many times in my life,

I took the easier way out because I knew I'd have a sure win. I believed I'd fail if I took the more difficult path. I deemed myself a failure and never gave myself a chance.

Whatever you're thinking, become aware of the thought, investigate it and then let it go if it doesn't apply. Thoughts aren't always rooted in truth.

YOU ARE YOU AND YOU ARE ENOUGH.

An Invitation to Act

1. *Thoughts impact how we feel and act. Become aware of what we are putting into our minds by keeping track of what you're thinking. Keep a thoughts log for one week. Whenever an event occurs that leads you to think negatively, write down that event, what you immediately thought and felt, and then what you did in response. Then ask yourself if the thought is true and write down an alternative response to the thoughts and outcome. Ex: I fail a test. My immediate thought is – I suck. I am a failure. My immediate feeling(s) – anger, disappointment, deflation. My outcome – I do not study for the next test because I have come to believe that I am a failure, so why should I bother studying? My subsequent failure becomes a self-fulfilling prophecy. My alternative response to the immediate thought and action is – Yeah, I failed the test because I did not study enough, not because I'm a failure. I can change the outcome by studying more next time.*

3

PHYSICAL

Millions of Americans make a New Year's resolution to lose weight. I am no exception. We start off with a bang and then by Valentine's Day, for a lot of us, we are back to being couch potatoes. Why does this happen? Well, the answer is simple – change is hard. It takes about 21 days for a change to become a habit. Many don't even stick it out that far. Fear is one of the main reasons people don't make a change. That is a shame because growth is on the other side of that change. Undergoing a physical change goes beyond just having a buff body and fitting into a new swimsuit. It is about loving yourself enough to care how your body operates so it can continue doing that for you for as long as possible. For many trauma survivors, body awareness and connection can be obstacles because we have learned how to disconnect our minds from our bodies to avoid the pain and the memories of the traumatic events that have happened to us. Dissociation is a common coping mechanism that is great for survival but not so great for daily living and functioning. When dissociation becomes our usual go-to to avoid discomfort, we miss out on the harmonious connection of our mind, body and spirit as well as the beauty and richness of life.

Aside from exercise, diet and avoidance of certain substances, taking care of our physical self extends to knowing our bodies in an intimate way. Are you in tune with your body? Are you aware of the signs your body sends to you? Do you recognize what happens to you physically when you're triggered? Do you pay attention to your gut when you sense something right or wrong? Our bodies talk to us daily. We just need to tune in.

Growth comes when we become aware of ourselves to the fullest extent possible. That includes the physical self. Over the next week or so, pay attention to how your body operates and what it senses. Take note of all five senses and write down what you experience, if you like. For trauma survivors, learning how to connect with the senses is a step toward integration. If this is too triggering for you, be sure to enlist the help of a mental health professional.

An Invitation to Act

1. *Try this 5-4-3-2-1 grounding exercise that helps you tune into your body and the present moment. First, pause and be still. If thoughts and feelings arise, that's okay. Just stay with them a little bit and ground into yourself. Then, find five things you can see. Notice as much detail about each object as you can. Next, find four things you can hear. Again, notice the details. Then, find three things you can touch and notice the details. Find two things you can smell. If you can't smell anything, imagine how a favorite item smells like. Finally, find one thing you can taste. If you can't taste anything, imagine how your favorite food or drink tastes. If you can't remember the order of the grounding exercise or what you should be doing with each sense, that's okay. Just do what you can. You may limit it to just three senses like sight, hearing and touch or even one sense like touch.*

2. *Engage in some type of body movement for at least five minutes. It could be dance, walking, running, swimming, yoga or whatever movement allows you to closely connect to the body as you move. You can do this on its own or incorporate the grounding exercise above to tune into how your body feels.*

4

EMOTIONAL

Emotional growth may be the hardest aspect to examine because it touches on feelings we sometimes don't understand or don't want to understand. We may want to avoid feeling at all. Protecting ourselves from ourselves is a good thing at times. It's the body's way of self-preservation. Dissociation is a common occurrence for trauma victims. To be fully present during a horrible event is too overwhelming for the body and the mind to comprehend, so often, the mind will disconnect you from your physical experience to protect you. Over time, you become disconnected and won't be able to grasp what you're feeling when it is safe for you to feel. You won't be able to recognize what it is that comes up for you as you go about your daily living. It is a lonely place to be.

Because of the potential for triggering, I strongly urge you to seek the services of a mental health professional to do the emotional work necessary to heal. You will need help recognizing feelings and putting a name to them. You will need guidance to find out what to do with all the feelings you may be experiencing now. Depending on what happened to you, buried memories will stir up feelings you may not be prepared to handle. It may be like a tsunami of emotions for you.

Please check the appendix for resources regarding seeking out mental health help.

YOU'RE DOING WONDERFULLY SO FAR.
KEEP GOING.

An Invitation to Act

1. *Consider finding a supportive mental health professional to assist you on your healing journey. Take as much time as you need in your search because it is profoundly important to locate someone who is the best fit for you. Also, ask the therapist if trauma is a specialty. Not all therapists have the training needed to handle clients with significant trauma in their background.*
2. *Try to incorporate breathing exercises into your self-care to help you regulate overwhelming emotions. The goal is not to avoid emotions – because all emotions are OK – but to learn how to navigate them when they arise so we are able to respond in a healthy way when triggered. What helps me is to put my hand on my heart, say a brief mantra like "I'm safe now," and slowly breathe in to a count of four. I then hold the breath for four, slowly release the breath to another count of four, hold that breath to a final count of four and repeat the cycle once or twice. That is my way but you may find something else that works better for you. There are numerous breathing exercises to do, so look to the internet for specific examples.*

5

SPIRITUAL

The life force, belief system and/or energy that gives you purpose, strength and the fuel to continue is your spiritual self. All beings have energy. All humans have intuition, which is what I call the sixth sense. You don't have to be religious or spiritual to discover or enhance that. It is the inexplicable 'something' that makes you *you.* Have you found it exists within you? Maybe you're still looking. All of that is okay. Spirituality is hard to define and is unique to each individual, so it's not like it'd be easy for me to describe what you should be looking for. If you engage your intuition, then you'll know you've touched the spiritual when that moment occurs.

Perhaps you're in a place where you shun anything and everything religious and/or spiritual because of a traumatic experience. There is such a thing as spiritual abuse. Anyone can fall prey to it, and any minister or clergyperson in power can be a perpetrator. It is one of the worst types of abuse because someone is taking advantage of your faith system and search for purpose. Searching for meaning, for something bigger than yourself, opens you up to being vulnerable and displaying weaknesses. When people in authority use those soft spots to satisfy their own lusts and destructive agendas, the violation is devastating. If that has happened to you, please let me tell you that whatever happened ***was not your fault***. Perhaps I'm the first person to tell you this. You are not to blame, and I hope you will achieve peace in knowing that. If you need the help of a psychotherapist, I suggest you look for someone who has special experience with helping spiritually abused victims, and be sure the person is a licensed, and preferably secular, professional. Anyone can call themselves a 'spiritual' or 'biblical' counselor because neither requires special training or education, and use their religious beliefs against you, which is another spiritual and emotional violation.

An Invitation to Act

1. *One way to tap into your intuition, which is part of your spiritual self, is to become attuned to your body. Pay attention to how it feels to be inside of it. Pay attention to when your body is thirsty, hungry, sleepy, emotional etc. Once you become aware of how your body feels, you'll be primed to pick up on the sixth sense of intuition. You'll be able to feel in your gut – sometimes literally – when things are right or wrong for you. You'll be able to just* **know** *without needing someone else's guidance about what you're feeling.*
2. *What does spirituality mean to you? Jot down what comes up for you in your journal.*

6

PERSEVERANCE

It is a new day. A day full of opportunities awaits you. How are you greeting it – like a domino or a pendulum? Dominos fall and don't get back up whereas a pendulum swings back and forth until purposely stopped. I hope you will want to be like a pendulum and maintain a steady movement as you go about your day regardless of what you do or whatever you encounter. If you have a wonderful day, then hooray for you! Keep going. If you have a horrible day, keep going. Recovery takes time and will be painful along the way as you encounter changes and stresses you've never faced before. But you must keep going.

I PROMISE BETTER DAYS ARE AHEAD.

An Invitation to Act

1. *Congratulate yourself for getting through the day. Listen to your body and ask it what it needs.*

7

TRUST

Today's meditation could've been a book-long piece on trust as it is probably the one issue with which trauma survivors struggle the most. There is no shame in not trusting anything or anyone. You have been through an ordeal that has stripped you of all decency, dignity and safety. You were used and abused. People you thought you could trust betrayed you. If your abuser was a family member, then your situation represented the ultimate violation of trust. Someone hurt you at your most vulnerable. So, it is quite understandable why you are hesitant and probably resistant to trusting. In my experience, I struggle with trust every day. I keep my intimate circle very small. It has taken me years to get to a point where I feel comfortable extending trust to someone, but there's always that moment of hesitation where I ask myself whether it's worth the risk. I don't think that hesitancy will ever go away.

However, building a wall around ourselves isn't healthy. Humans are made for connection and much research bears that out. When we reach out, we give a piece of ourselves, and that's why it's important to ensure we're giving trust to the right people. In a healthy relationship, romantic or otherwise, what we get in return should be just as fulfilling as what we're putting out. Anything less sets up the scene for a one-sided play. As trauma survivors, that is noteworthy. Our traumatized brains have been rewired to look for ways to fix the deficits gained from the traumatic experience. Subconsciously, we seek what we didn't get, and if we don't become aware of that tendency, the search could lead us to a place where we are re-traumatized. If you're attracted to emotionally unavailable people, narcissists (who are always emotionally unavailable), or others who suck the life energy from you (aka energy vampires), then you are trying to build a house on quicksand. Many of my relationships, romantic and platonic, were with people who fitted into those three categories. Growing up, I was never shown what a healthy relationship looked like, so I went looking for whatever I lacked.

Learning to trust again will be a slow process, and for many it will be a lifelong one. Take it one day at a time and be picky about who you trust.

YOU ARE WORTH IT.

An Invitation to Act

1. *Do you trust yourself and others? Are you surrounded by people who are trustworthy and emotionally available? If not, then this may be the time to examine your relationships. If you are in a situation involving domestic violence, then you should proceed with caution as taking action unsafely may put you in danger. Please see the Resources Section.*

8

NEGATIVITY

Humans are predestined to look for danger. It's a survival mechanism. Therefore, it's become much easier to find things that are going wrong or could go wrong more than it is to find something that's going right. Add trauma to our predestined inclinations and you have a recipe for a life ruled by negativity. As a victim, you had to look out for yourself as best you could and do whatever you needed to cope and survive. Now that you're in recovery and on the path to wellness, those same strategies may not be working out as well. Addictions and codependency come to my mind.

So, how can we break the cycle? Doing so involves more than just focusing on the positive and being happy all the time, which initially sounds like a good first step but in the long run skirts the core issue. Life has ups and downs for everyone, so to imagine a life without any difficulty whatsoever is unrealistic. So, what's the answer? Gratitude and meaning.

Research has shown that people who've survived traumatic events fared better when they (a) came to a place where they could focus on being grateful for what they had instead of focusing on what they didn't have and, (b) find a way to develop meaning after their experience. That focus does not diminish in any way the trauma that has happened. I also am not saying there was a purpose behind the trauma. What I am saying is finding meaning in your life post-trauma helps to instill hope and resilience. You are not your trauma and you don't have to let it define the rest of your life.

LOOK FOR SOMETHING TO HELP YOU MOVE FORWARD.

An Invitation to Act

1. *If you are able, read Viktor Frankl's book* "Man's Search for Meaning". *Frankl was a Holocaust survivor and psychologist who credited his survival to his discovery of meaning and purpose.*
2. *What do you think your purpose is in this world? Have you discovered it? If not, why not? Jot down your thoughts in your journal.*

9

POSITIVITY

We talked a lot about negativity in a previous meditation, so now is the time to focus on positivity. The point of this resource is supposed to be a positive one after all. Positivity is not forcing oneself to be happy all the time and glossing over problems. Positivity is an attitude one maintains despite the occurrence of negative events. It is so very tempting to remain negative, and our traumatized brains have been rewired to think that way, so fighting negativity can be an uphill battle.

How does one win the war against negativity? Mindfulness, disputation and gratitude. Let's say you have just gotten back an exam in which you scored 50 out of 100. Academically, 50 is a failing score. A negative thought pattern may look like this – *I failed the test. That means I'm stupid. I'm a failure. I always fail, so why bother trying anything?*

Using mindfulness, disputation and gratitude, the thought patterns can turn into this:

Yes, I failed the test. I feel stupid and ashamed. Those feelings are real and I honor them, but they are not rooted in truth. (Mindfulness)

Yes, I failed the test, but I have passed other tests and have succeeded at many other things, so I am not a failure. (Disputation)

I am grateful for this low score because it shows I need to prepare better for the next test. How can I prepare? What have I done in the past that has helped me? (Gratitude)

Do you see how negative thoughts can impact our feelings and actions? Thoughts, feelings and actions are interconnected. If you change your thoughts, then you are bound to change the other two aspects.

Another way to create a positive attitude is to surround ourselves with uplifting people, places and things. Why are substance abusers asked to avoid people, places and things from their old life? It is because those people, places or things probably contributed to a person's substance usage or are heavily associated with it. Those in recovery are at high risk for relapse unless they change their environment. It's awfully hard to avoid temptation when you're surrounded by it. A changed person can make others uncomfortable about their own issues, so, because misery loves company, they will encourage the recovering user to reuse. Maintaining contact with positive support systems is a key factor in recovery.

The same holds true for trauma survivors. Negativity breeds negativity. If you find yourself having a difficult road to recovery, then you may want to look at who is around you. Are you surrounded by supportive, healthy people who are encouraging you? Or, are you around people who zap the life energy out of you and don't do anything to help your progress? This examination of your environment will be tough. In fact, it may be brutal. It's hard to say goodbye, especially if it's someone to whom you've become particularly attached.

Some trauma survivors are paralyzed by Stockholm Syndrome or domestic violence dynamics, which makes it difficult to leave.

For those who may be unfamiliar with the term, Stockholm Syndrome is a psychological phenomenon in which a trauma victim bonds with the abusers and may even sympathize with them.

A note for domestic violence victims: Only you can decide when it's time to leave. Before you do so, please make sure you have a plan in place that ensures your safety and that of others who may be leaving with you. Please check Resources Section for more information.

THOUGHTS, FEELINGS AND ACTIONS ARE INTERCONNECTED.

An Invitation to Act

1. *What helps you stay positive? Are you supported in your efforts or do you feel you're doing this alone?*
2. *Try the thought-reversal process outlined in this meditation. Whenever a negative event happens, note the initial thought and feeling that arise as well as the resulting action. Find a way to dispute the thought and jot it down.*

10

IDENTITY

Changes have been occurring in your life. If they've been coming quickly, they may upset your sense of self. Who am I now that this and that have changed?

Perhaps you never knew who you were to begin with. That is entirely possible if all you've ever known is pain and suffering. Child abuse victims come to my mind initially, as do victims of human trafficking. It is hard to make sense of what happened let alone try to figure out who you are now that the traumatic event has stopped.

Part of the growth process you're undergoing as you become well includes discovering who you are. What makes you *you*? What do you like and dislike? What makes you sad? What makes you happy? You will come to learn the answers to those questions and more. You will also discover who you are now in the wake of the trauma that has occurred. What does your life look like now that you're trying to become well? Many layers of hurt have to be unearthed before you can find answers. It is a time for patience.

As you discover who you are, you will grow stronger in your sense of self and become more confident.

THE PERSON YOU'RE MEANT TO BE WILL BE REVEALED IN TIME.

An Invitation to Act

1. *Who are you? For at least 20 minutes, write down the answer. If you can't think of anything or become stuck while writing, jot down what you are thinking currently or repeat the previous statements you've written. Or you can make a list. If you go beyond the 20 minutes, that's OK.*
2. *Make four short lists. On the first list, write down 5-10 qualities you think you have. On the second list, write down 5-10 qualities others have said you have. On the third list, write down 5-10 things you like. On the fourth list, write down 5-10 things you don't like. Compare the lists. Are there any connections or patterns? Are there are items that really grab your attention? If so, highlight those items.*

11

BOUNDARIES

You have a right to establish a boundary to protect yourself. You have a right to say no. No is such a beautiful word. There's never anything wrong with saying no to anything that threatens your peace.

However, imposing certain boundaries on yourself can be problematic. In an effort to protect yourself, have you put limits on what you can and can't do thus inhibiting your growth? Are you using the word 'can't' a lot?

If you are, don't be ashamed for doing so. Anxiety, fear and negative self-talk do a number on our self-esteem. Plus, if you've been around someone who has said repeatedly, *You're worthless, stupid, and a failure,* then you may have that soundtrack running in your mind. Lies can turn into truth if you hear them long enough.

The person you were before the trauma is not the person you are now. You've done some incredible and wonderful things to get to this point in your life. And the fact you're reading this book tells me you know you can accomplish more. You just need some encouragement, which I hope this book is giving you.

Boundaries are meant for property not people when it comes to achieving recovery and fulfilling purpose. Courage has helped you get this far. Hope will take you the rest of the way. You've started a plan to heal, and it's starting to feel good. Why would you put limits on that process? And once you're solidly in your recovery, you will need boldness to take you to the next chapter of your story.

**YOU HAVE A LIFE PLAN AND PURPOSE.
DON'T BOX YOURSELF IN. KEEP GOING.**

An Invitation to Act

1. *Try to go one day without saying the word 'can't.' If 24 hours is too much, then aim for something more doable like 15 minutes, 30 minutes or an hour. Do whatever you can.*
2. *Consider writing down a mantra or two about possibility or ability as they pertain to you. Here are some examples of mantras I've used: 1. I can do this! 2. Strive for progress not perfection! 3. I got me!*

12

SHARING

In the meditation on trust, we talked about how difficult it can be for trauma victims to trust because of their histories of severe betrayal and others' lack of understanding. Sharing makes you vulnerable because you're exposing a part of yourself to someone else. Like love, sharing is a risk, one that has to be discerned very carefully.

You may not be ready to share. That's fine. Someone destroyed your trust. You have every right to take your time in building it back up again. You may also be asking yourself whether a particular person is safe. Tons of articles on the internet address that topic but let me share with you some of what I've found to work in discerning who is safe.

1. *Is the person open and authentic?* If this person is asking you to open yourself up while he/she/they remain closed, then be careful. A trusting relationship relies on openness and authenticity. The exception to this is within certain professional relationships. For example, a mental health professional has ethical reasons for not disclosing certain personal facts. After all, therapy is for the client not the therapist. A true professional knows when to self-disclose to build trust.

2. *Has the person lied to you?* Real relationships are built on honesty. If someone can't be honest with you, run for the nearest exit and don't look back.
3. *Is the person empathic?* Finding someone who listens well and is willing to walk the journey with you – and not for you – is a hard search. You've been through a horrible experience and deserve to have someone caring, compassionate and patient by your side.
4. *Has the person demanded you trust them?* Trust needs to be earned, and given your history, that will take a lot longer than perhaps it would with others. An empathic and understanding person will understand this.
5. *Is the person discreet?* If this person is blabbing your information to others, then do not under any circumstances tell this person a single thing. The exception to this is a mental health or medical professional who, when the circumstances arise, is ethically and legally bound to report to appropriate authorities. Clients and patients are to be told this at the beginning of their treatment.

Sharing, under the right circumstances, can be a wonderful and profound experience.

IT IS SO EMPOWERING TO FIND SOMEONE TO WHOM YOU CAN TALK.

An Invitation to Act

1. *Do you have a safe person with whom you can share? If so, think about the qualities that make this person safe. If not, think about the qualities needed before you can confide in them.*

13

SELF-ACCEPTANCE

Today, I'd like you to take a good long look in the mirror. What do you see? Your mind may focus first on what you perceive as imperfections – frown lines, wrinkles, gray hair, body fat, etc. Whatever it is, I ask that you ignore those features for a moment and look a little deeper. Is it possible that a warrior survivor could be staring right back at you? You may not feel like that at the present moment, but that doesn't make it any less true. The fact you are up and staring in the mirror tells me you can entertain the reality that you are a good and valuable person. The fact you are even reading this book tells me you are a fighter who hasn't given up and wants to use whatever resources you can to find hope for a better day. **YOU ARE A SURVIVOR.**

Though the world, especially the media, may tell you differently, you are acceptable **JUST AS YOU ARE. YOU ARE ENOUGH!!!!** You are meant for a purpose. Our traumatized brains won't accept this affirmation at first, so we must keep fighting. We must find a way to push that message through until we accept it.

HEALING BEGINS WITH SELF-ACCEPTANCE OF WHO YOU ARE AT THAT MOMENT.

An Invitation to Act

1. *One way to practice self-acceptance is to connect with your divine source via prayer or meditation. Look on the internet to find prayer and meditation videos, talks and apps. I personally like the Calm app. Acceptance is achievable but will take practice.*

14

SELF-CARE

If you have been seeing a mental health professional, perhaps you're familiar with the term 'self-care.' Its meaning goes beyond taking care of the basic hygienic needs. Self-care refers to ways of putting yourself first so your physical, emotional and mental well-being is preserved. The way it manifests is different for each person. Setting a boundary between what your responsibilities are versus that of another is a form of self-care. Saying no is self-care. Taking time out to decompress by walking, sleeping, vacationing etc. is self-care. Whatever makes you feel safe, supported and nurtured is self-care.

Why is self-care important? If we don't take care of ourselves, we will not be able to heal in the way we need to do. We won't be able to help others either. You can't give if your tank is empty.

As a survivor, the concept of self-care may be foreign to you because you've been told for so long that your needs aren't valuable and that you don't matter. Well, I'm here to tell you that you ***do*** matter. You are a beautiful creation of the universe who is unique with unrepeatable gifts, talents and abilities. You may not be at a point yet where you've discovered what those are but I know they're there because every single person on this planet has them.

THERE'S ONLY ONE YOU IN THE WHOLE WIDE WORLD, SO TAKE CARE OF YOURSELF.

An Invitation to Act

1. *What does self-care look like for you? Have you ever engaged in it? If so, how was the experience? If not, why haven't you engaged in it? Take a moment to jot down your thoughts.*
2. *Take five minutes starting today to engage in self-care. It doesn't have to be a huge or expensive thing. It could be as simple as taking an extra five minutes in the shower or sleeping in a little bit. Once you've taken the five minutes, try to extend that time daily and schedule it on your calendar. You are important enough to be an appointment on your calendar!*

15

OBSTACLES

Our traumatized brains tend to be in survivor mode – fight, flight, freeze or fawn – to maintain our balance. We are always looking for dangers and threats. The search is constant. We've been trained to be this way for so long that it's hard to imagine being something else. Each day brings its own set of challenges and obstacles. It's hard to let our guard down. And oh so exhausting!

When it seems to you that there are insurmountable obstacles ahead and you start getting overwhelmed, remember to stay in the present. Being mindful about where we are and what we're doing at any given moment helps to relax us and lowers the heart rate and blood pressure. If you're in a place where you feel safe, try this exercise. You may keep your eyes open or closed. Take your time as you follow each step. The idea is to relax, not finish in record time. First, pause and take a slow, deep breath and then release it slowly. Do that a few times until you feel a little calmer. Then, notice five things you can see. Don't think beyond what you observe. If a thought pops into your head, just use one word like 'thought' or 'thinking' and then let it go. Second, notice five things you can hear. Again, if a thought pops into your head, observe it and then let it go. Third, notice five things you can smell. Fourth, notice five things you can taste. A thought may happen. If so, let it float by and continue. Fifth, notice five things you can touch. After you've noticed these things, take a deep breath and open your eyes if you've kept them closed. You should be feeling less anxious and more relaxed. If not, try the exercise again.

Obstacles, like thoughts, seem insurmountable, but with a little creativity and a moment to pause, you will find they're fleeting.

YOU ARE NOT YOUR THOUGHTS NOR YOUR OBSTACLES.

An Invitation to Act

1. *Try the grounding exercise outlined in the meditation at least once this week. There are other variations of this exercise like 5-4-3-2-1 or 3-2-1. Do whatever feels comfortable for you and don't worry if you forget the sequence. The point is to become grounded in the moment and release the current stress you're feeling.*

16

FEAR

FEAR – FALSE EVENTS APPEARING REAL

Fear is real and imaginary. Our brains are designed to detect danger to keep us alive. In a healthy brain, alerts are based on truly dangerous and fear-inducing circumstances, such as an impending car crash or an armed robber entering a bank. In a traumatized brain, alerts are based on events masquerading as threats. Someone who has experienced trauma and is suffering from post-traumatic stress will see ordinary events as threats. One example is someone misinterpreting the sound of a car backfiring for a bomb exploding. Our brain gets tricked into thinking certain occurrences are threats and sets our bodies in motion to respond to the potential danger. Fight, flight, freeze or fawn is our response. Brains that have been damaged by tragic circumstances are difficult but not impossible to heal. As healing occurs, new neural paths are created in the brain that retrain it to resume healthy activity. It takes a long time for this to happen, but it does occur nonetheless. If you want to gain a fuller understanding of how trauma affects the brain, look up some of the work by trauma and neuroscience experts like Dr Bessel van der Kolk or Dr Dan Siegel *(see Resources)*.

Addressing your fears is a key component to wellness. Avoiding anything that puts you into a fearful state provides temporary relief but prolongs misery because you're only repressing the very fear you need to face. The next time around, the fear will resurface and come back stronger. It creates an automatic response that is hard to overcome. The best way to address fear is to face it – head on. Facing the fear will make you uncomfortable and you will want to escape, which is why it's important to involve a mental health professional in your recovery. You will need someone who's trained to help you walk through the fire to face your demons and offer emotional support as you do it.

DON'T LET FEAR GET IN THE WAY OF YOUR RECOVERY. YOU HAVE COME TOO FAR TO LET GO NOW.

An Invitation to Act

1. *Consider getting a copy of Dr van der Kolk's book "The Body Keeps the Score." It is a solid resource on learning how trauma impacts the brain and body and one of the few books I recommend to my clients who have experienced traumatic stress.*
2. *Consider finding a competent mental health professional to help you navigate your responses to fear-based triggers.*

17

LOSS

Missing aspects of our hurtful experience is a common and understandable feeling. Being in an unhealthy place brings a sense of comfort if that environment is all we've ever known. Change is scary. The fear of all the unknowns can be overwhelming. So, leaving that place is a loss. If you're experiencing these feelings, don't be ashamed by them. Feelings are feelings. There's no right or wrong to them. You are entitled to your feelings, so remember to accept whatever emotion arises and then let it go.

Trauma steals our identities and in a lot of cases, our innocence, our childhood and our opportunities. It is okay to mourn those losses too. The person you were before the trauma is not who you are now, and it's normal to miss that person. You may also be feeling anger and sadness, which is normal.

These are just a few of the losses to be experienced after a trauma. As you consider your losses, remember to be gentle with yourself and avoid self-blame. Regardless of what happened, you are not to blame. *You are not to blame.*

GRIEVE WHAT YOU HAVE LOST.

An Invitation to Act

1. *Consider a way to acknowledge and honor the losses you've experienced. Some ways to do this are making a collage with images representing what was lost, writing in a journal about the losses, lighting a candle or even holding a private ritual or ceremony.*

18

TIMING

You are right where you need to be at this moment. The universe's timing is perfect. A second earlier would've been too soon and a second later would've been too late. Don't rush through the moment that's meant for you right now.

It is hard to wait when you want something so badly, like wellness. You've been hurting for so long and just want relief. But the healing process can't be rushed. Each day you learn something new about yourself that sets up the foundation for tomorrow's lesson. Rushing that process eliminates possibilities to grow and decreases presence. Just being could be all that's needed for that particular moment.

I often wonder why it took me decades to reach a place where I felt like I had some semblance of healing. I think it did because I wasn't ready to face what had happened to me and when I did finally confront it, I wanted to rush through the process because I had seen how quickly others seemed to recover, and to be honest, I just didn't want to experience the pain that comes with feelings. The key word there is 'seemed.' I was only assuming others were racing ahead of me. I had no clue how long they had been working toward wellness. I eventually learned to be wary of comparisons. Others' journeys were different from mine, just as mine will be different from yours. I am still healing. Like so many intangible things in life, there is no timeline. You will progress at your own pace.

YOUR TIMING WILL BE PERFECT FOR YOU AND NOBODY ELSE.

An Invitation to Act

1. *Take a moment to appreciate where you are in your healing journey right now and how far you have progressed. Even if you've just begun, you are farther along than you were yesterday.*
2. *Give yourself a hug.*

19

HONESTY

Honesty is a form of kindness that you extend yourself to help maximize your recovery. No healing can occur without looking at yourself and your situation in a realistic and honest way. In today's reading, I'd like you to take a closer look at your environment. Are you in a positive environment that will allow you to recover? Are you surrounding yourself with people who will propel you toward integration?

If you've just gotten out of a traumatic experience, like a domestic violence situation, then your leaving is a huge step forward into a new life. It takes courage to leave when you don't know what's going to happen next. In fact, that's one of the reasons why many people stay in such relationships because they fear the unknown and they often have no resources to start anew. At least you knew what to expect by being with your abuser. Leaving a toxic environment gives you a fresh start and freedom to discover who you are without having to seek approval from someone who may not have your best interests at heart.

Honesty also involves examining why you were in that situation in the first place. I am not blaming the victim but merely reiterating my point made earlier about gravitating toward something unhealthy because our traumatized brains are wired to do that. If you were to look at your life, would you find any patterns? History repeats itself when we haven't avoided the pitfalls of the past because we never realized they were there in the first place. Exploring the past may bring up triggers and emotions you may not be prepared to handle, so I strongly recommend you seek the help of a mental health professional for this part of your recovery journey.

An Invitation to Act

1. *Where are you? Who is with you? Take a few minutes to determine whether you're in a place that will enable growth and wellness. If you are not, it may be time to consider a way to bring you to a safer place physically, mentally and emotionally.*

20

KNOWLEDGE

One of the hardest parts of recovery is we have to face our pain. We have to know why we are hurting so much. We have to know how to heal. Knowledge is power but without application it is useless. You may discover many things but what key pieces of knowledge will actively help you in your wellness? I'd say self-awareness is one. Self-compassion is another. Whatever we find out about ourselves and our world, we have to know how to apply it to our everyday lives. In my experience, the death of my father, who was my main abuser, was the catalyst for deep introspection and my journey to become a therapist. I had to learn to know myself and be comfortable with what I found before I could extend myself to others. I hope your journey will enable you to have similar discoveries.

TO KNOW THYSELF IS THE BEGINNING OF WISDOM

– SOCRATES.

An Invitation to Act

1. *What obstacles prevent you from knowing more about yourself and your life?*
2. *How can you overcome those obstacles?*

21

CHOICE

When the level of discomfort is more than you can stand, you have a choice to make. One, get away from the discomfort. Two, stick with it and learn to cope with the discomfort. Or three, learn how to transform the discomfort to something positive. Each choice has positive and negative consequences.

Perhaps you've faced a choice like that in which there was no easy or desirable answer. What did you do and how did you go about it? Could whatever you've learned from that experience be applied to your current situation of recovery?

Once you've made your choice, the next difficult step is accepting the decision. This may be awfully hard to do if you've chosen to do something others wouldn't have done. For example, in a lot of domestic violence cases, the abused partner often decides to stay with the abuser. There are myriad reasons for this; economics, fear, low self-esteem and lack of support are just a few. However, it is important to remember that we aren't living in someone else's shoes. We don't have to live with the impact of a choice someone else made, so we shouldn't judge what they've decided to do. We can only control what ***we*** do, say and think.

Making a choice is heroic for someone who hasn't had the power to make one previously. Even more courageous is sticking with that choice.

A note for domestic violence victims: If you're in a situation mentioned above where you've decided to stay with your abuser, then I wish you well. Though the odds are stacked against you that you'll be safe, only you can decide what is best for you and your family. Please refer to the Resources Section should you decide to leave and need help.

An Invitation to Act

1. *If you feel comfortable doing so, think about a time in which you had to make a difficult choice. How did you make that choice and what happened in the aftermath? Is there anything from that experience that you can apply to your current situation?*

22

UNIQUENESS

Do you know what makes you you? Uniqueness. There hasn't been anyone just like you before in this world and there will never be anyone else like you after you leave. The distinct and unrepeatable presence you offer to the world is a gift. Your life is a gift. You matter.

I know this may be hard to believe. As a survivor, how many times have you been told that you don't matter, that nobody cares about you, that your life is worthless? A lie told often enough starts to sound like the truth, but it is not! Regardless of what you look like and what you've done, you are a beautiful creation of the Universe. You are loved and are worthy to be loved. It may take a long time to believe these statements, and that's okay. This whole journey is made of baby steps. However long it takes, it takes. Once you start believing you're unique, you're loved and you can contribute in some way, you will feel better about yourself.

If you want, make a list of all the qualities that make you unique. Talents, gifts, physical attributes, personality traits, etc. Everyone has something special about them and it doesn't always mean it's something huge. Not everyone can be an actor or a politician.

Maybe you are always looking out for others or you make an awesome apple pie. Maybe your smile lights up the room and your personality makes others look forward to being around you. Whatever it is, find it because it's in there and it deserves to be recognized.

CELEBRATE YOUR UNIQUENESS! STAND PROUD AND BE WHO YOU ARE, THE PERSON YOU WERE MEANT TO BE.

An Invitation to Act

1. *Write a list of items you like about yourself. If you can only think of one thing, then that's OK. Write it down. Second, write a list of positive statements others have said about you. Third, write a list of ways you have helped yourself and others. Review the lists and circle or highlight the items that catch your attention or hold special meaning for you. Post the lists in a place where you will frequently see them like a bedroom, bathroom mirror or refrigerator door.*

23

KINDNESS

Today's meditation is similar to a previous one on self-care in that I will encourage you to take care of yourself in ways that go beyond taking care of basic human needs. It differs in that I will ask you to go a little deeper as you look within yourself and consider how kindness is a type of self-care. When we are kind to ourselves, we show honor and respect to the creation made by the Divine One. We understand we only have one body, mind and spirit and that uniqueness is deserving of love and care.

Kindness to self is also about setting boundaries with ourselves and others. Boundaries make us feel emotionally and physically safe. Boundaries protect the values, beliefs and principles we've created to live a life with meaning and integrity.

Kindness is about being brave enough to be honest with yourself. If you're just beginning your journey you may not be ready to do this, and that's okay. Early in recovery, it's more important to gain a sense of safety and trust. However, if you're a veteran healer, then it may be time to dig a little deeper to reach the next step in your recovery. Take a hard look at yourself and ask yourself these questions: Have you been doing all you can to recover? If not, why? If so, is there anything else you can do? While we are not responsible for our trauma, we do share responsibility in our healing.

These are difficult questions, and I don't ask them to instill guilt or shame. Trauma is like a poison that seeps into every crack of our being and it takes heart-wrenching work to get all of it out. Unresolved issues will come back to haunt you. It is a kindness to do as much as you can to find a way to rid yourself of the poison trauma inflicts because you deserve to be well. That way may lie in psychotherapy and support groups, or it may be in meditation, prayer, exercise or some other healthy practice. There is no one way that will work for everyone.

BE KIND TO YOURSELF.

An Invitation to Act

1. *Think about the ways you are extending kindness to yourself. If you are not, then ask yourself why.*

24

BELIEF

Belief. Sticking with something because we know it's real and true. But how do we know it? We can feel it with our senses. Or we just *know.* Belief can be difficult to define and defend because we don't always have something tangible to back it up.

With the right manipulation, we can turn belief into doubt. In abusive relationships, this is called gaslighting. For example, let's say someone makes rude and insulting jokes to your face and you call them out on it. You know you heard what you heard because you were standing right there in front of the person as they made those hurtful comments. But the person says to you, "Oh, you're so sensitive. I was only joking. You must've taken it the wrong way or misheard me." The other person is so convincing and sincere as they say this to you that you begin to have doubts. After a few situations like this, you start to second-guess yourself and ask – *Did what I just experience happen? Maybe it really was all in my head.* You start to disbelieve your reality. That is gaslighting.

You will know you're growing in this area when you're able to stand by what you experience and believe in your own senses. Seeds of doubt will wash away as you grow stronger and more attuned to your intuition.

Trauma survivors are especially vulnerable to this phenomenon because they become disconnected to their reality to avoid further psychological pain because they've been physically, emotionally and mentally beaten into submission by their circumstances. A lie becomes the truth when heard often enough and then internalized.

Remember that everything you've experienced is real and it did happen to you. Do not let anyone tell you otherwise.

GIVE POWER TO YOUR BELIEF.

An Invitation to Act

1. *Belief rests in the mind and body. To stand in our truth, we have to become aware of it and trust it. One way to do that is to learn how to tap into your mind and body. Embodiment techniques (dance, yoga etc.) and meditation are excellent conduits for the messages our bodies want to communicate. Consider taking up a meditation or embodiment practice.*
2. *Practice breathing and grounding techniques. The quieter you become, the easier it will be for your mind and body to communicate with you.*

25

MINDFULNESS

Have you ever been so preoccupied while driving that you find yourself suddenly realizing you have no recollection of how you got to your destination? That's happened to me a few times and it's scary. It's so easy to go on autopilot when your mind is full of thoughts. I have missed out on so many wondrous moments because I've been focused elsewhere. Then, I discovered the wonderful concept of mindfulness. Mindfulness is a way of being intentional and attentive at the same time. You are paying attention to what you're doing at the moment and fully register and notice all facets of that experience. Mindfulness is the gateway to awareness, appreciation and application.

Imagine this experience. You're seated enjoying your favorite hot drink. Notice the mug you chose to contain your beverage. Is it colorful? Is it chunky? Is there a message on it that resonates with you? Was the mug a gift? Feel the mug and notice whether it's smooth, rough or maybe even chipped.

Now take a look at your beverage. Watch how the steam dances above the mug. Notice the color of your drink and the richness of the browns, blacks or whatever color your beverage may be. Maybe it has a creamy tinge to it if you added something to it.

Then as you drink it, notice how it tastes and flows down your throat. Revel in the perfection of the moment. You are alive and enjoying a wonderful hot mug of your favorite drink. A simple pleasure but so delectable.

Mindfulness involves using all your senses to take in moments of your day and finding ways to appreciate them for what they are. You will never have that second, minute or hour again.

A LIFETIME IS BUILT UPON MOMENTS LIKE THESE, SO ENJOY THEM WHILE YOU CAN.

An Invitation to Act

1. *Find another experience to practice mindfulness. Perhaps it could be while you're reading this book. Pause and take in everything your senses bring to you.*

26

PRESENCE

Presence, like mindfulness, is touching base with all your senses in the current moment. You are experiencing and noticing everything in that moment without distraction. The focus is on the here and now. Paying attention to the present is a way to alleviate anxiety as well as give thanks for the blessings therein.

In a world full of distractions, staying focused on whatever we are doing is a challenge, but practicing presence will reap rewards like clarity, intentionality and concentration. Presence also improves relationships because you stay focused on yourself and the other person as you interact. Without presence, creating connections is difficult if not impossible.

One way to focus on the present is doing a breathing exercise. There are exercises galore to do, but one of my favorites goes as follows: First, sit in a comfortable chair, place your hands on your knees and try to relax your muscles as best as you can while keeping your head, neck and back upright. Then close your eyes or, if you prefer, keep them open and find something upon which to focus with a soft gaze. Inhale deeply and slowly count to 10. Keep your focus on your breath. When you get to 10, hold your breath for a second or two and then slowly exhale through your mouth with your lips slightly parted to a count of 10. Repeat.

As you do this exercise, keep your attention on the breath. If a thought pops into your head, accept it, let it go and come back to the breath.

Another way I find that helps me stay focused on whatever I'm doing is to take a deep breath and say a little mantra, "I'm here. Be all here." This comes in pretty handy when I'm seeing clients all day, many times in back-to-back sessions. It helps me prepare and bolster my attention so I can focus on whoever I'm helping. My clients deserve my attention and presence.

If breathing and mantras aren't your thing, then take a second and stare at one thing in front of you. Maintain your normal breathing. Notice the color, shape and details of whatever you're staring at. Don't let any detail go unnoticed. After 30 seconds to a minute of this, you should feel calmer and more focused.

I'M HERE. BE ALL HERE

An Invitation to Act

1. *How are you present in your life? What helps to maintain that presence?*
2. *For at least one time over the course of the day, practice any of the exercises mentioned above or another you've found to be helpful.*

27

UPLIFTING

What have you found to be uplifting in your life? For me, I am moved by a great song on my playlist with meaningful lyrics and a catchy beat. Chocolate uplifts me. So does taking a walk on the wooded trail by my neighborhood. Writing, of course, is an uplifter. Faith and friends are also strong supports.

Trying to find positivity in a negative situation can be challenging, and it can be nearly impossible to find something good and positive that takes us out of our misery. We survivors have been inundated with negativity on too many occasions and have developed coping mechanisms to get us by.

When I was a child, I bit my fingernails down to nearly the quick to cope with all the anxiety I felt growing up in a home where abuse was omnipresent. I felt the need to be perfect to avoid drawing negative attention, so I became an overachiever and chewed my nails to deal with the stress of everything I was trying to handle. My other coping mechanisms were eating and picking my skin. As I grew, the nail biting stopped as did the skin picking, but not the eating. Then, I discovered retail therapy, and you can probably guess how that turned out for me.

Replacement behaviors are only bandages on the wound. They don't cure them. I share that with you to let you know you're not alone. We have all used various coping mechanisms that helped us endure and survive whatever we experienced. There is no shame in that.

However, at some point we must come to terms with the consequences of those choices when they begin to interfere with our daily functioning. When the discomfort exceeds the comfort, we are faced with a choice.

KEEP SEARCHING FOR POSITIVE AND UPLIFTING SOURCES THAT WILL SOOTHE YOUR MIND, BODY AND SPIRIT.

An Invitation to Act

1. *What coping mechanisms did you use to survive? Are they the ones helping you now live a healthy life?*
2. *What uplifts you?*

28

MERCY

The word 'mercy,' like many words in the English language, has Latin roots and is defined as having compassion for someone with all of one's heart. While mercy is something most typically extended to someone else, I say it can also be applied to oneself. Have you shown yourself mercy?

It is common for trauma victims to blame themselves for what happened to them, even if that something was a natural disaster or an accident. Even those who have not experienced trauma can fall prey to this anytime something negative happens. Questions or thoughts that often swirl around in the head are: Did I do something wrong? Should I have done that? Maybe if I hadn't been there or done that, then this wouldn't have happened. I made them do that, so I'm to blame.

If you're having these thoughts now, be merciful to yourself and stop. Regardless of what happened, you are not to blame. You didn't cause the tornado to happen. You didn't cause someone to abuse you. You didn't cause your trauma. Your experience is what happened **TO** you, not by you.

It takes practice to switch those thoughts around, and that's where a mental health professional can step in and help you by using cognitive behavioral techniques. It will take time to understand what you're thinking and why, and even more time to develop strategies to combat automatic negative thinking.

REMEMBER,
YOU ARE NOT TO BLAME!

An Invitation to Act

1. *Have you shown mercy to yourself? If so, what was that experience like? If not, what would help you extend mercy to yourself? Be honest.*

29

SELF-LOVE

In the previous meditation, I discussed being merciful to yourself, which is a form of self-love. Now, I'm going to take a deeper dive into this concept of self-love. Loving yourself is putting your own interests first and doing what's best for you whether it's taking care of yourself, setting a boundary, leaving a toxic environment or pursuing a goal. Loving yourself is seeing yourself as you are and accepting what you see, imperfections and all. Loving yourself is agreeing to change yourself for your own reasons if you so desire, not anyone else's. If you cannot love yourself, you will not be able to love anyone else in the way they deserve. How can you value others if you don't value yourself?

It is easier for trauma victims to hate themselves than love. That hate partly lies in a belief they should've done something to prevent whatever happened to them. Hate also lies in the shame many victims have from experiencing a pleasurable bodily response while being abused (e.g., when a sexually abused victim becomes physically aroused or has an orgasm during the abuse). It rests in the internalized messages received from someone who've said you're disgusting, unworthy, ugly, hateful, mean etc. They learn to equate the event to their identity and come to believe the bad thing happened because they are bad people.

If you've been with someone who is an abuser, you may have been told that you're being selfish for focusing on yourself instead of that person. I'm here to tell you it is not selfish to love yourself. An abuser says that to protect their own interests and exert control. Abuse victims tend to push aside their own desires and needs to satisfy the abuser because they have no other choice. Acquiesce to the demands or be hit...raped...killed. They are used to giving while the abuser is used to taking. Now that you're healing, know that it is not selfish to turn the tables around and focus on yourself for once. Humans can only neglect themselves for so long before the body breaks down. If you don't pay attention to your wellness, you will be forced to pay attention to your illness.

An example of the importance of self-love is shown every time you fly. Before takeoff, a flight attendant demonstrates the procedure for obtaining more oxygen should the plane lose cabin pressure. Travelers are told to *put their own oxygen mask on first* before they help someone else, like a child in their charge. If you can't breathe, you will not be able to help someone else. The same concept applies here – put your own oxygen mask on first to help yourself, and perhaps others someday.

LOVE IS SELF-ISH, BUT NOT SELFISH.

An Invitation to Act

1. *Ask yourself if you love yourself. Be honest.*
2. *If you do love yourself, how do you demonstrate that love? If you don't, what is one small step you can take* ***today*** *to show yourself love?*

30

HOPE

True healing can't happen without hope. A hope that you can make it through the day. A hope that tomorrow will be a better day. A hope that you'll be better than you were yesterday. A hope that you can achieve your dreams. Hope is what concentration camp survivors like Elie Wiesel and Viktor Frankl clung onto that kept them alive. Humans need hope.

The trauma experience extinguishes hope for many. Years of being beaten in body, mind and spirit will do that. So, when you find yourself on the other side of that experience, having hope is quite a new thing to have. Hope grows as your trust, confidence and self-love develop. What you've previously seen as impossible turns into "I'm possible." You are a valuable human being who deserves hope. I hope you will see that for yourself one day.

HOPE GROWS AS YOUR TRUST, CONFIDENCE AND SELF-LOVE DEVELOP.

An Invitation to Act

1. *Write this down and post it someplace visible to you – H.O.P.E. =* **Hold On Pain Ends**
2. *Think about what gives you hope.*

31

PEACE

As we near the end of this book, I hope you are finding this to be just as worthwhile to read as it's been for me to write. I also hope you are beginning to experience a sense of peace.

Have you ever been mesmerized by the sight of a babbling brook? Water flowing serenely over rocks, moss and dirt, making small noises here and there yet never straying from its course. The water keeps flowing in the same direction though a rainstorm may make it swell here and there. Imagine you're the water and life is the rainstorm. Downpours will come. How will you handle them? I'm hoping you will go with the flow and stay the course toward wholehearted healing.

Eventually, in your recovery you will discover a type of serenity that allows you to maintain your emotional well-being regardless of what happens around or to you. Peace. In Christian circles, this peace that surpasses all understanding is discussed in Philippians 4:7. That biblical meaning is certainly applicable to anyone regardless of your religious or spiritual persuasion. If you don't get caught up in the worries of today and understand that everything passes, you will discover this peace that will keep you calm regardless of your circumstances.

Terrible things have happened to you. I don't want to minimize that fact. But in order to heal, you must acknowledge it, accept it and then move on. Don't let your life be defined by your trauma. As long as you stay rooted in what hurt you, you will never achieve peace and realize the person you are meant to be. And that would truly be a shame because the world needs you.

YOU MATTER. YOU ARE WORTHY. YOU ARE LOVED. PEACE BE WITH YOU.

An Invitation to Act

1. *What brings you peace? What has helped develop peace for you?*
2. *Heal and be you!*

32

FINAL THOUGHTS

I hope you have found a sense of hope, peace, awareness and love while reading it. It has been nothing short of joy to write this as my way of giving back. This book has become the person I needed growing up.

This book may have stirred up unexpected thoughts and feelings, so, in the days, weeks and months to follow, I ask that you be gentle with yourself. It takes time to understand new information and longer still to process it. Reread sections if you need to do that. Do whatever feels right for you in the moment to help you. You may want to reach out to a trusted friend, mentor or mental health professional during this time for additional support.

If you believe you've received as much as you need from this book, please feel free to share it with someone in your circle. Spreading knowledge is an integral way to create a ripple effect.

A Resources Section follows to help you wherever you are in your healing journey. The list is not all inclusive, but it is a good starting point.

If you are a domestic violence victim, I ask that you think and plan carefully if you've decided to leave and consult with a helping professional for guidance.

BE STILL, BE BOLD
AND BE WELL.

RESOURCES

On Trauma

- Dr Daniel Siegel: Prominent psychiatrist, author and creator of the concept of interpersonal neurobiology which centers on the brain's role in holistic well-being. Find out more about him at www.drdan-siegel.com .
- Dr Bessel van der Kolk: Prominent psychiatrist, author and researcher on trauma. He wrote the New York Times' bestselling book, *The Body Keeps The Score*, which addresses the impact of trauma on the body. You can learn more about him at www.besselvan-derkolk.com .

On Domestic Violence & Abuse

- Deaf Abused Women's Network (DAWN): 202-559-5366, hot-line@deafdawn.org, www.deafdawn.org
- Domestic Violence Initiative (for the differently abled): 1-877-839-5510, www.dviforwomen.org
- National Child Abuse Hotline/Childhelp: 1-800-422-4453, www.childhelp.org
- National Coalition Against Domestic Violence: www.ncadv.org
- National Dating Abuse Helpline (U.S.): 1-866-331-9474, www.loveis-respect.org
- National Domestic Violence Hotline (U.S.): 1-800-799-SAFE (7233), TTY = 1-800-787-3224, www.thehotline.org
- National Human Trafficking Resource Center/Hotline (operated by The Polaris Project): 1-888-373-7888, text HELP to BeFree (233733), www.polarisproject.org
- National Sexual Assault Hotline: 1-800-656-4673, www.rainn.org

- Women of Color Network: 1-800-537-2238, www.wocninc.org

On Mental Health

- Crisis Text Line: Text "Hello" to 741741
- National Alliance on Mental Illness (NAMI): 1-800-950-6264 or info@nami.org . NAMI Helpline can be reached Monday through Friday 10 a.m. to 6 p.m. ET.
- National Center on Domestic Violence, Trauma & Mental Health: 1-312-726-7020, ext. 2011, www.nationalcenterdvtraumamh.org
- National Suicide Prevention Lifeline: 1-800-273-8255, www.suicide-preventionlifeline.org
- Psychology Today: Contains a directory of mental health professionals, www.psychologytoday.com . A word of caution – sometimes the provider listing can be out of date so make sure to contact them first to see if they are accepting clients.
- Substance Abuse and Mental Health Services Administration (SAMHSA): 1-800-662-4357
- Veterans Crisis Line: 1-800-273-TALK and press 1 or text 838255
- Your insurance provider: Contact your carrier to check on two items – 1. Whether you have mental health coverage and what that stipulates; 2. What providers are in your area. Many providers offer the option of self-pay or sliding scale fees.

About the Author

Lori A. Peters is a licensed counselor in Pennsylvania, resilience coach and writer. She earned her Bachelor of Arts degree in journalism from Penn State University and her Master of Science degree in clinical mental health counseling from Shippensburg University. Lori has worked with dozens of adults, teens and children. Her clinical specialties include trauma, grief and mood disorders.

CPSIA information can be obtained
at www.ICGtesting.com
Printed in the USA
BVHW042104231221
624755BV00013B/907